Teen Violence Workbook

Facilitator Reproducible Self-Assessments, Exercises & Educational Handouts

Ester A. Leutenberg

John J. Liptak, EdD

Illustrated by

Amy L. Brodsky, LISW-S

wholeperson
Stress & Wellness Publishers
Duluth, Minnesota

Whole Person
210 West Michigan Street
Duluth, MN 55802-1908

800-247-6789

books@wholeperson.com
www.wholeperson.com

Teen Violence Workbook
Facilitator Reproducible Self-Assessments,
Exercises & Educational Handouts

Printed in the United States of America

10 9 8 7 6 5 4 3 2 1

Editorial Director: Carlene Sippola
Art Director: Joy Morgan Dey

Library of Congress Control Number: 2012955824
ISBN: 978-1-57025-270-9

Using This Book *(For the professional)*

Teen violence can break out at anywhere and at any time. The question of why teens become violent has been thoroughly researched and studied. Unfortunately, pinpointing the exact causes of teen violence is complex. Some of the potential causes include the following:

- Teens tend to model behavior – When teens see violent acts by family members at home, actors in the movies, in video games they play, by gang members in their communities, by bullies at school, and on the Internet, they are often inclined to replicate such behaviors, believing those behaviors are the "norm." This social learning theory suggests that most behaviors are learned through observation and modeling.

- Teens often have difficulty in appropriately channeling their frustrations and therefore lash out in anger. These frustrations can include being bullied in school, having a disability, not being able to do well in school, feeling pressured by peers to do things they don't want to do and/or experiencing pressure from parents to succeed.

- Teens often become enraged and seek revenge on those who bully or hurt them. Some teens, tired of being bullied or abused, simply lash out in revenge.

- Teens often react with self-destructive behaviors, especially those with low self-esteem or with family problems. They are at risk for using drugs or alcohol, having unprotected sex, depression, eating disorders, violence and suicidal ideation.

What constitutes violent behavior?

Violent behavior in teens can include a wide range of behaviors including: explosive temper tantrums, date rape, physical aggression, school shootings, suicide, bullying, fighting, threats or attempts to hurt themselves and/or others (including homicidal thoughts), use of weapons, cruelty toward animals, fire setting, and intentional destruction of property.

What are the risk factors?

Violent behavior is unique to each individual, so it is difficult to list specific risk factors. Some behaviors that suggest violent behavior is imminent include antisocial beliefs and behaviors, use of drugs and alcohol, gang involvement, lack of commitment to school, victimization by others through teasing or bullying, poor anger management and conflict resolution skills, and interpersonal problems. This violence can happen at home, school, on a date – anywhere at any time.

Reporting

Stress the following points to participants:

- Do not to tell a person you are reporting abuse, just report it. People who are being abused will thank you later.

- Women are crying out on social networks for help to talk about domestic violence. They may not be able to report abuse and violence due to fear of retaliation.

- If you know of someone who is experiencing domestic violence, please know that YOU anonymously can help by calling the Domestic Violence Hotline 1–800–799–SAFE (7233).

- The suicide rate for people with domestic violence is high and this is a problem often ignored on social networks.

(Continued on the next page)

Using This Book *(For the professional, continued)*

The *Teen Violence Workbook* contains seven separate sections that will help participants learn more about themselves as well as the impact on their interpersonal relationships and the quality of their lives. Participants will develop a new awareness of the violence that they are exposed to daily. They will complete assessments and activities to help them explore the violence in their lives and develop strategies for coping with violence.

SECTIONS OF THIS BOOK

1) **Types of Abuse Scale** helps teens explore the types of abuse they are experiencing in their relationships. The scale includes physical/psychological abuse, verbal/emotional abuse, sexual abuse and financial abuse.

2) **Self-Empowerment Scale** helps teens explore their personal level of power to avoid or reject violent acts.

3) **Experiencing Dating Violence Scale** helps teens identify harmful beliefs about dating relationships that their partners possess.

4) **Potential for Violence Scale** helps teens determine their potential for becoming abusive in their dating relationships.

5) **Personal Safety Scale** helps teens examine how cautious they are in order to remain safe in an often violent society.

6) **Symptoms of Violence Scale** helps teens explore the signs related to violence, and determine what type(s) of violence they are experiencing in their life.

7) **Safety Plan** helps teens develop a personalized plan for their safety and the safety of their oved ones.

By combining reflective assessment and journaling, participants will be exposed to a powerful method of verbalizing and writing to reflect on and solve problems. Participants will become more aware of personal strengths and areas requiring growth and improvement of their daily life skills.

Preparation for using the assessments and activities in this book is important. The authors suggest that prior to administering any of the assessments in this book, you complete them yourself. This will familiarize you with the format of the assessments, the scoring directions, the interpretation guides and the journaling activities. Although the assessments are designed to be self-administered, scored and interpreted, this familiarity will help prepare facilitators to answer participants' questions about the assessments.

Use Name Codes for Confidentiality

Confidentiality is a term for any action that preserves the privacy of other people. Because teens completing the activities in this workbook are asked to answer assessment items and to journal about and explore their relationships, you will need to discuss confidentiality before you begin using the materials in this workbook. Maintaining confidentiality is extremely important as it shows respect for others and allows participants to explore their feelings without hurting anyone's feelings or fearing gossip, harm or retribution.

In order to maintain confidentiality, explain to the participants that they need to assign a name code for each person they write about as they complete the various activities in the workbook. For example, a friend named Joey who enjoys going to hockey games might be titled LHG (Loves Hockey Games) for a particular exercise. In order to protect their friends' identities, they may not use people's actual names or initials, just name codes.

The Assessments, Journaling Activities and Educational Handouts

The Assessments, Journaling Activities, and Educational Handouts in the *Teen Violence Workbook* are reproducible and ready to be photocopied for participants' use. Assessments (scales) contained in this book focus on self-reported data and can be used by psychologists, counselors, therapists, teachers and others in the helping professions. Accuracy and usefulness of the information provided is dependent on the truthful information that each participant provides through self-examination. By being honest, participants help themselves to learn about unproductive and ineffective behavior patterns, and to uncover information that might be keeping them from being as happy and/or as successful as they could be.

An assessment instrument can provide participants with valuable information about themselves; however, it cannot measure or identify everything about them. The purpose of an assessment is not to pigeon-hole certain characteristics, but rather to allow participants to explore all of their characteristics. This book contains self-assessments, not tests. Tests measure knowledge or whether something is right or wrong. For the assessments in this book, there are no right or wrong answers. These assessments ask for personal opinions or attitudes about a topic of importance in the participant's life.

When administering assessments in this workbook, remember that the items are generically written so that they will be applicable to a wide variety of teens; however violence cannot account for every possible variable for every teen. Use assessments to help participants identify possible negative themes in their lives and find ways to break the hold that these patterns and their effects have.

Advise the teens taking the assessments that they should not spend too much time trying to analyze the content of the questions; their initial response will most likely be true. Regardless of individual scores, encourage teens to talk about their findings and their feelings pertaining to what they have discovered about themselves. Talking about and working on practical life skills will improve their quality of life as well as assist them in developing positive interpersonal skills to self-access throughout life. These exercises can be used by group facilitators working with any teens who want to strengthen their overall wellness.

A particular score on any assessment does not guarantee a participant's level of life skills. Use discretion when using any of the information or feedback provided in this workbook. The use of these assessments should not be substituted for consultation and wellness planning with a health care professional.

Thanks to the following professionals whose input in this book has been so valuable!

Carol Butler, MS Ed, RN, C
Annette Damien, MS, PPS
Beth Jennings, CTEC Counselor
Hannah Lavoie
Jay L. Leutenberg
Kathy Liptak, Ed.D.
Eileen Regen, M.Ed., CJE

Adding Variety by Using Physical Movement
Contributed by Carol Butler, MS Ed, RN, C

Teens tire of sitting, reading and writing. The following activities correspond with the chapters and can be done after a brief discussion of each topic.

Chapter 1 – Types of Abuse

Help teens identify different types of abuse by printing four signs:

Physical / Psychological, Verbal / Emotional, Sexual, and Financial.

Place a sign on each of the four walls of the room. A volunteer reads randomly, (mixing up the order of items), from the lists on pages 18 and 19, items 1-40. Teens stand under the sign that signifies the type of abuse described. Alternately, teens can describe a real life experience and peers will stand under the sign that signifies the type of abuse they think was described. Emphasize there are no right or wrong answers if teens can substantiate their decisions.

Chapter 2 – Self Empowerment Scale

Place a continuum on the board, (or on the floor with masking tape); label it with numbers 1-10 and write "LOW" under #1 and "HIGH" under #10. Ask teens to position themselves under the continuum on the board, (or on the continuum on the floor), to show where they are regarding their level of self-empowerment and explain why. Teens then brainstorm how each participant might move closer to the "10" HIGH, by changing thoughts and behaviors.

Chapter 3 – Experiencing Dating Violence

Help teens identify types of violence by printing four signs: Jealousy, Control, Lifestyle, and Abusive Behavior. Place a sign on each of the four walls of the room. A volunteer reads randomly, (mixing up the order of items), from lists on pages 48 and 49. Teens stand under the sign that signifies the type of violence described. Alternately, teens can describe a real life experience and peers will stand under the sign that signifies the type of violence they think was described. Emphasize there are no right or wrong answers if teens can substantiate their decisions.

Chapter 4 – Potential for Violence

Place a continuum on the board, (or on the floor with masking tape); label it with numbers 1-10 and write LOW under #1 and HIGH under #10. Ask teens to position themselves under the continuum on the board (or on the continuum on the floor) to show their level of risk for violent behavior toward others and explain why. Teens brainstorm how each participant might move closer to the #1 LOW, by changing thoughts and behaviors or getting help with issues (anger, jealousy, control, lifestyle, etc.).

Chapter 5 – Personal Safety Scale

Seven teens take turns writing one of the following on the board and then eliciting and listing peers' related safety ideas: Home, School, Work and Volunteering, Dating and Relationships, Community, Cyberspace and Driving.

(Continued of the next page)

Adding Variety by Using Physical Movement *(Continued)*

Chapter 6 – Symptoms from Experiencing Violence Scale

Print the following on the board in random, scattered order, not in lists, rows, or columns:

Detachment, Physical Symptoms, Cognitive, Emotional, Stay in the Present, Aerobic Exercise, Low Intensity Exercise, Affirmations, Music, Visualization, Thought Stopping, Proper Breathing, Progressive Relaxation, Meditation, Nutrition, Simple Pleasures, and Quotations.

Teens take turns being blindfolded and walking up to the board (with a volunteer who ensures their safety). They touch a spot on the board, remove the blindfold, and elaborate on or demonstrate the word or phrase closest to where their finger landed. If they are unfamiliar with the term, peers assist. They may refer to the information in the chapter also.

Chapter 7 – Safety Plan

Post a sign with the one of the following labels on each of four walls: 1) Supportive Agencies and People; 2) Safe Places and Get-Away Kit; 3) Helping Siblings, Relatives and Friends; 4) School-People, Nearby Places, and Getting Home. Teens divide into four panels, huddle under their chosen or assigned sign, discuss ideas amongst themselves and then share with the whole group.

They may refer to the information in the chapter or use the worksheets as guides.

Alternately, write each of the four topics as a heading on four large pieces of chart paper; post one onto each of four walls. Teens walk around the room writing ideas on each paper.

Pantomimes for Chapter 1 and Chapter 3

Pairs or trios of teens can pantomime, while peers guess what they types of abuse or violence they are portraying. Use caution with physical and/or sexual movements. Teens should check with the facilitator before doing their non-verbal enactments!

See examples below:

- Without touching, one partner prepares to punch the other by clenching a fist. One can pretend to throw something at the other or to pour a drink in the partner's face. (*Physical / Psychological*)
- One partner shakes a finger in the other's face and moves his/her mouth as if yelling. (*Verbal*)
- One person glares at the other in a suggestive way or makes hugging and kissing motions without actual contact) as the other puts up hands as if to say "Go away" or "Back off." (*Sexual*)
- One person puts out his/her palm and points into it forcefully; the other pretends to pull out a wallet and put a wad if money in the other's hand. (*Financial*)
- Two teens are talking; a third pulls his/her partner away; one constantly calls/texts the other. (*Jealousy*)
- Using body language, a partner tells the other to sit here, stand over there, to jump up and down, and slightly and safely, to bend over backward. (*Control*)
- One teen portrays drinking or injecting or smoking drugs. (*Lifestyle*)
- One teen shows mood swings with facial expression and body language by smiling one minute, crying the next, hitting a wall the next. (*Abusive Behavior*)

Layout of the Book

The *Teen Violence Workbook* is designed to be used either independently or as part of an integrated curriculum. You may administer one of the assessments and the journaling exercises to an individual or a group with whom you are working, or you may administer a number of the assessments over one or more days.

This book includes a combination of the following reproducible pages in the seven sections:

- **Assessment Instruments** – Self-assessment inventories with scoring directions and interpretation materials. Group facilitators can choose one or more of the activities relevant to their participants.
- **Activity Handouts** – Practical questions and activities that prompt self-reflection and promote self-understanding. These questions and activities foster introspection and promote pro-social behaviors.
- **Quotations** – Quotations are used in each section to provide insight and promote reflection.
- Participants will be asked to select one or more of the quotations and journal about what the quotations mean to them.
- **Reflective Questions for Journaling** – Self-exploration activities and journaling exercises specific to each assessment to enhance self-discovery, learning and healing.
- **Educational Handouts** – Handouts designed to enhance instruction can be used individually or in groups to promote a positive responsibility for safety at home, in the classroom, and in the community. They can be distributed, scanned and converted into masters for overheads or transparencies, projected or written on boards and/or discussed.

Who Should Use This Program?

This book has been designed as a practical tool to help professionals, such as therapists, school counselors, psychologists, teachers, group leaders, etc. Depending on the role of the professional using the *Teen Violence Workbook* and the specific group's needs, these sections can be used individually or combined for a more comprehensive approach.

Why Use Self-Assessments?

Self-assessments are important in responding to various teen life skills issues because they help participants to engage in these ways:

- Become aware of the primary motivators that guide their behaviors
- Explore and learn to set aside troublesome habits and behavioral patterns
- Explore the effects of unconscious childhood messages
- Gain insight and a wake-up call for behavioral changes
- Focus participants' thinking on behavioral goals for positive changes
- Uncover inner resources participants possess that can help them to cope better with modes of personal safety
- Explore personal characteristics without judgment
- Develop full awareness of personal strengths and areas in need of growth

Because the assessments are presented in a straightforward and easy-to-use format, individuals can self-administer, score and interpret each assessment at their own pace.

Teen Introduction

Teens live in a society of violence. It can be difficult to avoid. Following are some suggestions for reducing violence in your life:

Make a commitment to be non-violent yourself. Do not bully, tease, ridicule, malign or spread negative gossip about others. It is important to respect others and value their differences. One way to do so is to broaden your social circle to include others who are different from you.

Learn to manage your anger. Learn ways to resolve arguments and fights without violence and ways to engage in calm negotiation and compromise. Encourage your friends to do the same.

Get involved in your school and community. Participate in extra-curricular programs. Look for such activities as volunteering with a community group, playing sports, writing, playing a musical instrument, or joining a club or any after-school program.

Avoid alcohol and drugs. Attempt to stay away from alcohol and drugs as well as people who use them. There is a strong link between the use of alcohol and drugs and violence.

Do not carry a gun or other weapons. Contrary to popular belief, carrying a gun to protect yourself will not make you safer. Guns simply escalate the level of conflict and increase the chances that you will be seriously harmed. If someone is threatening you and you feel that you are in serious danger, confide in an adult you can trust. Discuss your fears or contact school administrators or the police.

Be cautious. Take precautions for your safety. For example: avoid. Stay with a group of friends or trusted adult.

If you know someone is planning to harm someone else, report this person and the situation to an appropriate, trusted adult. If you know someone is in danger, tell a trusted adult, such as a teacher, guidance counselor, principal or parent. If you are afraid and believe that telling will put you in danger or lead to retaliation, find a way to anonymously contact the appropriate authority. If you know of someone experiencing domestic violence, please know that YOU anonymously can help by calling the Domestic Violence Hotline 1–800–799–SAFE (7233). The suicide rate for people with domestic violence is high and this is a problem often ignored on social networks.

The good news is that if you are either being violent or experiencing violence, this book can help you. Many people are not even aware of the patterns and triggers for their violent actions. The *Teen Violence Workbook* relies on a self-reflective method that is therapeutic, educational and non-threatening. It is designed to help you learn about the various types of violence and how exposed you are to violence in many areas of your life, and learn ways to deal with your violent behaviors and/or violence at home, in school, on a job, in your relationships and community.

Confidentiality

You will be asked to respond to assessments and exercises, and to journal about some experiences in your life. Everyone has the right to confidentiality, and you need to honor the right of everyone's privacy. Think about it this way – you would not want someone writing things about you that other people could read. Your friends, family and acquaintances feel this way also.

In order to maintain the confidentiality of your friends, assign people code names based on things you know about them. For example, a friend named Sherry who loves to wear purple might be coded as AWP (Always Wears Purple). **Do not use any person's actual name or initials when you are listing people – use only name codes.**

Teen Violence Workbook
TABLE OF CONTENTS

TABLE OF CONTENTS

TABLE OF CONTENTS

TABLE OF CONTENTS

SECTION I:
Types of Abuse Scale

Name_____

Date_____

Types of Abuse Directions

Teen violence is not limited to physical abuse such as bullying or school shootings. Many different forms of violence surround teens: physical / psychological abuse, verbal / emotional abuse, sexual abuse and financial abuse. In addition, many victims of abuse are often harmed in more than one of these ways at the same time. The Types of Abuse Scale can help you identify the different types of abuse and violence that you may be experiencing.

This assessment contains forty statements. Read each of the statements and decide if the statement is true or false. If it is true, circle the word **True** next to the statement. If the statement is false, circle the word **False** next to the statement. Ignore the numbers after the True and False choices. They are for scoring purposes and will be used later. Complete all forty items before going back to score this scale.

In the following example, the circled False indicates that the item is false for the participant completing the Types of Abuse Scale:

I . In my family, school and community there is a person who ...

1. Pushes, shoves, slaps, punches, bites, chokes, burns,
pulls my hair and / or throws objects at me . . . . True (1) (False (0)) Score _____

This is not a test and there are no right or wrong answers. Do not spend too much time thinking about your answers. Your initial response will be the most true for you.
Be sure to respond to every statement.

(Turn to the next page and begin)

Types of Abuse Scale

I . In my family, school and community there is a person who ...

1. Pushes, shoves, slaps, punches, bites, chokes, burns,
   pulls my hair and/or throws objects at me . . . . True (1)   False (0)   Score _____

2. Blames me for his/her anger . . . . True (1)   False (0)   Score _____

3. Tries to run my life . . . . True (1)   False (0)   Score _____

4. Isolates me . . . . True (1)   False (0)   Score _____

5. Threatens to harm him/herself if I leave . . . . True (1)   False (0)   Score _____

6. Abandons me in dangerous situations . . . . True (1)   False (0)   Score _____

7. Tells me who I can and cannot be friends with . . . . True (1)   False (0)   Score _____

8. Threatens me with weapons . . . . True (1)   False (0)   Score _____

9. Requires me to get permission before
   doing anything . . . . True (1)   False (0)   Score _____

10. Goes through my belongings without
    my permission . . . . True (1)   False (0)   Score _____

TOTAL _____

II. In my family, school and community there is a person who ...

11. Ignores my feelings . . . . True (1)   False (0)   Score _____

12. Ridicules and/or insults me . . . . True (1)   False (0)   Score _____

13. Pressures me to use alcohol, drugs,
    or cigarettes . . . . True (1)   False (0)   Score _____

14. Ridicules and insults my values and beliefs . . . . . True (1)   False (0)   Score _____

15. Rarely approves of what I do . . . . True (1)   False (0)   Score _____

16. Threatens to get me in trouble . . . . True (1)   False (0)   Score _____

17. Tries to influence all of my important decisions. . . . True (1)   False (0)   Score _____

18. Threatens to leave, break up or
    abandon me regularly . . . . True (1)   False (0)   Score _____

19. Pressures me to quit activities I like to do . . . . True (1)   False (0)   Score _____

20. Wants to control me . . . . True (1)   False (0)   Score _____

TOTAL _____

(Continued on the next page)

Types of Abuse Scale *(continued)*

III. In my family, school and community there is a person who ...

21. Likes me for my body only . . . . True (1)   False (0)   Score _____

22. Makes me wear certain clothing against my will . . . True (1)   False (0)   Score _____

23. Criticizes my sexuality . . . . True (1)   False (0)   Score _____

24. Touches me when and where I do not
    want to be touched . . . . True (1)   False (0)   Score _____

25. Withholds affection from me . . . . True (1)   False (0)   Score _____

26. Compares me to other relationships . . . . True (1)   False (0)   Score _____

27. Shows sexual interest in others in public . . . . True (1)   False (0)   Score _____

28. Threatens to tell people about what
    we have done . . . . True (1)   False (0)   Score _____

29. Forces me to have sex against my will . . . . True (1)   False (0)   Score _____

30. Commits aggressive or forceful sexual acts . . . . . . True (1)   False (0)   Score _____

TOTAL _____

IV. In my family, school and community there is a person who ...

31. Does not help to support me financially . . . . True (1)   False (0)   Score _____

32. Does not help support our family financially . . . . . . True (1)   False (0)   Score _____

33. Takes my money away from me . . . . True (1)   False (0)   Score _____

34. Forbids me to earn or spend my own money . . . . True (1)   False (0)   Score _____

35. Neglects to provide me with what I need . . . . True (1)   False (0)   Score _____

36. Takes and spends any money I earn . . . . True (1)   False (0)   Score _____

37. Does all of the banking, even though I want to . . . . True (1)   False (0)   Score _____

38. Asks me to justify all of my purchases . . . . True (1)   False (0)   Score _____

39. Controls all family income and assets . . . . True (1)   False (0)   Score _____

40. Denies me money for necessities . . . . True (1)   False (0)   Score _____

TOTAL _____

(Go to the Scoring Directions on the next page)

Types of Abuse Scale
Scoring Directions

The Types of Abuse Scale is designed to help you to explore the different ways that you may be experiencing abuse in your life. To score this scale, you need to determine your scores on each of the individual scales and for the overall Types of Abuse total.

To score the Types of Abuse Scale look at the 40 items you just completed, focus on the numbers after each choice rather than the **True** or **False**. Total your score for each section. Use the spaces below to transfer your scores to each of the scales below.

I.   **Physical / Psychological Abuse Scale**   Total Score _____

II. **Verbal / Emotional Abuse Scale**   Total Score _____

III. **Sexual Abuse Scale**   Total Score _____

IV. **Financial Abuse Scale**   Total Score _____

Profile Interpretation

Individual Scale Score	Total Scores	Result	Indications
0 to 1	0 to 9	very low/ none	You are experiencing very little or no abuse at this time, however, ANY amount of abuse is not okay!
2 to 4	10 to 19	low	You are experiencing some abuse at this time.
5 to 7	20 to 29	moderate	You are experiencing a moderate amount of abuse at this time.
8 to 10	30 to 40	high	You are experiencing a great deal of abuse at this time.

The higher your score on the Types of Abuse Scale, the more you might be experiencing that type of abuse. In the areas in which you score in the **Moderate** or **High** range,

make efforts to ensure that you are safe and have a plan prepared to escape the violence if necessary. No matter if you scored **Low**, **Moderate** or **High**, the exercises and activities that follow are designed to help you to develop a comprehensive plan for ensuring your safety and possibly that of a family member.

Physical and/or Psychological Abuse

People scoring high on this scale are currently exposed to physical and/or psychological abuse. Physical violence is the intentional use of physical force. Sometimes it can cause injury, disability or even death, but physical violence does not need to cause physical injury in order to be abuse. Physical abuse can include any form of unwanted physical contact, such as hitting, burning, biting, shoving, throwing, punching, kicking or restraining. Psychological abuse includes threats of physical violence with or without weapons or any behaviors that cause you to feel less independent.

Who is the person? (use name code)	What does the person do?	What can you do about it?

Verbal and/or Emotional Abuse

People scoring high on this scale are currently exposed to verbal and emotional violence. Verbal and/or emotional violence can include verbal threats of physical violence, humiliation, name-calling, continual blaming, withholding information, ridiculing or embarrassing the victim, and isolating a person from family and friends.

Who is the person? (use name code)	What does the person do?	What can you do about it?

Sexual Abuse

People scoring high on this scale are currently exposed to someone who uses physical force to coerce them to engage in sexual intercourse or sexual acts against their will. Sexual abuse can include pursuing sexual activity when you are not fully conscious, when you are not asked for consent, or you have said no, or are afraid to say no, or aggressive or forceful physical contact.

Who is the person? (use name code)	What does the person do?	What can you do about it?

Financial Abuse

People scoring high on this scale are currently exposed to financial or economic abuse. The abuser has control over your money and other economic resources. Financial abuse includes withholding money for necessities, making you account for every penny spent of your earnings, forcing you to beg for money, preventing you from working or from finishing or obtaining education, and/or stealing your money.

Who is the person? (use name code)	What does the person do?	What can you do about it?

Abuse

Describe the abuse you have experienced in the past or are presently experiencing? (use name codes)

_____

_____

_____

_____

_____

_____

_____

How does the person who has abused you, or is presently abusing you, justify the abuse?

_____

_____

_____

_____

_____

_____

_____

What have you done about it or what will you do about it?

_____

_____

_____

_____

_____

_____

SECTION II:
Self-Empowerment Scale

Name_____

Date_____

Self-Empowerment Scale
Directions

Self-empowerment is a critical aspect in overcoming any violence. Self-empowerment is about acting in your own best interest and promoting your long-term well-being. It is about being able to overcome violence you may have experienced in the past and avoid it in the future. The Self-Empowerment Scale was designed to help you examine if you are successfully moving on from any violence you have experienced and living the life you have always dreamed of living.

This assessment contains 40 statements that are related to you and your current life. Read each of the statements and decide whether or not the statement describes you. If the statement is **TRUE**, circle the number next to that item under the **TRUE** column. If the statement is **FALSE**, circle the number next to that item under the **FALSE** column.

In the following example, the circled number under FALSE indicates the statement is not true of the person completing the inventory.

	TRUE	FALSE
I have a general lack of confidence.	1	(2)

This is not a test. Since there are no right or wrong answers, do not spend too much time thinking about your answers. Be sure to respond to every statement.

(Turn to the next page and begin)

Self-Empowerment Scale

	TRUE	FALSE
I have a general lack of confidence	1	2
My self-esteem is as good as most other people's self-esteem	2	1
I feel powerless and victimized	1	2
I feel as if I am unlovable	1	2
I don't measure up to my peers	1	2
I have great skills and abilities	2	1
I often feel inferior to other people	1	2
I like my appearance	2	1
I put myself in dead-end relationships	1	2
I am not isolated socially	2	1

A – TOTAL _____

	TRUE	FALSE
I feel as if I can never get anything right	1	2
When criticized, I evaluate whether the critics are correct	2	1
I feel that others value who I am	2	1
I don't try to live up to unrealistic expectations . . . , . , ...	2	1
I am always being criticized for what I do or say	1	2
If someone corrects me, it devastates me	1	2
I set realistic goals for myself	2	1
I worry about being criticized	1	2
I am my own hardest critic	1	2
I will not do things if I think others will criticize me for it	1	2

B – TOTAL _____

(Continued on the next page)

© 2013 WHOLE PERSON ASSOCIATES, 210 WEST MICHIGAN ST., DULUTH MN 55802-1908 ▪ 800-247-6789

Self-Empowerment Scale *(Continued)*

	TRUE	FALSE
I have spent most of my time taking care of other people.	1	2
I can be assertive when I want to be	2	1
I work hard to make sure that others don't become angry	1	2
I try to anticipate and avoid disapproval	1	2
I place others' needs above my own	1	2
I am afraid to hurt the feelings of others	1	2
I am not afraid to express a differing opinion	2	1
I am not as assertive as I could be	1	2
I have trouble telling people what I want	1	2
I am not hesitant to tell people how I feel	2	1

C – TOTAL _____

	TRUE	FALSE
I do things that I normally wouldn't do if someone asks	1	2
I do things to fit in with my friends	1	2
I don't do anything that I feel I should not do	2	1
I let others pressure me to do things	1	2
I do things to show others I can	1	2
I do things to be accepted	1	2
I am my own person	2	1
I do things so that others don't think badly of me	1	2
I will not be pressured to do something that I don't want to do	2	1
I go along with the crowd	1	2

D – TOTAL _____

(Go to the Scoring Directions on the next page)

Self-Empowerment Scale
Scoring Directions

The Self-Empowerment Scale is designed to measure whether or not you feel empowered and are your own best self-advocate.

To calculate your score, total the numbers that you circled for each of the sections. They will range from 10 to 20. Put that number in the space marked.

A – LOW SELF-ESTEEM TOTAL   =   _____

B – CRITICISM TOTAL   =   _____

C – WANTS & NEEDS TOTAL   =   _____

D – PEER PRESSURE TOTAL   =   _____

To get your overall self-empowerment score, add the four scores above. Your overall score will range from 40 to 80. Put your total score in the space below:

SELF-EMPOWERMENT TOTAL   =   _____

Profile Interpretation

Individual Scale Scores	Total Scales Scores	Result	Indications
17 to 20	67 to 80	High	A high score suggests that you tend to have high self-esteem, are not hurt by criticism, express your wants and needs, and are not swayed by peer pressure. You are your own best self-advocate.
14 to 16	54 to 66	Moderate	You feel somewhat empowered. You have some work still to do.
10 to 13	40 to 53	Low	A low score suggests that you may lack self-esteem, feel self-critical, have difficulty expressing your wants and needs, and often are swayed by peer pressure.

For scales which you scored in the **Moderate** or **Low** range, find the descriptions on the pages that follow. Then, read the description and complete the exercises that are included. No matter how you scored, low, moderate or high, you will benefit from all of these exercises.

Self-Empowerment Scale Descriptions

A – LOW SELF-ESTEEM

People scoring low on the *Low Self-Esteem Scale* often have a low opinion of their self-worth. They often do not want to get up and out on time in the morning. They often pull away from others and isolate themselves. They feel a general lack of self-control and self-confidence. They feel inadequate, unlovable and powerless.

B – CRITICISM

People scoring low on the *Criticism Scale* feel as if they are constantly being criticized. Because you are consistently bombarded by negative criticism from your parents and peers, you begin to internalize the words and believe them, whether they are true or not. You have a negative view of yourself and have little respect for others. You are also your own harshest critic.

C – WANTS & NEEDS

People scoring low on the *Wants & Needs Scale* often are not as assertive as they should be. Assertiveness is at the very heart of empowerment. Assertiveness is about asking for what you want and not tolerating disrespect from your partner. Assertiveness is responding effectively to aggression, clearly communicating your wants and needs, and refusing unreasonable requests.

D – PEER PRESSURE

People scoring low on the *Peer Pressure Scale* tend to want to go along with the crowd. They feel it is important to fit in with their peer group and allow themselves to be pressured to be accepted. Often they do things they wouldn't ordinarily do, because the actions do not fit in with their personal values.

Self-Empowerment Scale

Regardless of your score on the assessment, the following exercises have been designed to help you learn more about empowerment in the teen violence cycle. The following exercises are designed to help you capitalize on your strengths and overcome your weaknesses.

Increasing Your Self-Esteem

All people experience feelings of low self-esteem from time to time. It is normal to do so. However, if you have been abused, low self-esteem may be a constant state of mind for you. Low self-esteem sometimes comes from years of being told that you are unworthy, you never do anything right, and you are a bad person. You may even be convinced that the abuse was your fault. You may know deep inside that these things are not true, but it's hard to let go of those feelings. To increase your self-esteem, complete the exercises that follow.

In the spaces below, list things that help you feel as if you are a good, valuable person:

I AM A GOOD, VALUABLE PERSON
Example: I love my grandmother very much and like to read to her at least once a week.

My Positive Self

What kinds of positive statements do you, or can you, make about yourself? In the spaces below list some of the things you like about yourself.

Don't be modest!

In school, I am proud of _____

_____

_____

_____

_____

In my family I _____

_____

_____

_____

_____

I am most proud of myself because _____

_____

_____

_____

_____

I am unique in these ways:_____

_____

_____

_____

_____

I am respectful of_____

_____

_____

_____

_____

(Continued on the next page)

My Positive Self *(Continued)*

I feel successful when _____

_____

_____

_____

At my work or volunteer place I_____

_____

_____

_____

In school I am good at_____

_____

_____

_____

I am respected for_____

_____

_____

_____

One of my personality traits is _____

_____

_____

_____

I like this about myself:

_____

_____

_____

_____

_____

_____

I am Tough on Myself

Teens are often their own greatest critics.

In the spaces below, list all of the ways that you are hard on yourself.

Areas of My Life	How I Am Tough on Myself?	How I Can Give Myself a Break?
Example: School	*I want all A's.*	*I don't need to be perfect.*
School		
Home/Family		
Work/Volunteer		
Social Life		
Friends		
Other		

When Others Are Critical

Teens are often criticized by others. In the spaces below, list the ways that others are tough on you. (use name codes)

Areas of My Life	Who Is Critical of Me?	How Are They Critical?
Home/Family		
School		
Work/Volunteer		
Social Life		
Friends		
Other		

Your Wants and Needs

Assertive people are able to express their desires, needs and wants.

This takes some practice.

What I Want

To assert yourself, you must know what you want. By establishing what it is that you really want, you will be able to assert yourself when you need to. You will know what is worth fighting for and what to simply walk away from. In each of the boxes below, list what you want in each of the categories. (use name code)

From	I Want
Example: My boyfriend or girlfriend	*I want MGF to listen to me and treat me respectfully.*
My boyfriend or girlfriend	
My teacher(s)	
A certain relative	
My friends	
Other	

Non-Assertive Situations

It is helpful to identify those situations in which you need to be more assertive. By becoming more aware of those situations in which you are not assertive, you can practice your assertiveness training skills. For each of the situations listed below, describe how you show a lack of assertiveness.

Situations in Which I Lack Assertiveness	Why I Am Non-Assertive	What I Can Do to Be More Assertive
Saying no to others		
Asking for favors		
Disagreeing with others' opinions		
Taking charge of a situation		
Social situations		
Asking for something I want		
Stating opinions		
Asking for help		
Dating situations		
Asking for time by myself		
Speaking in front of groups		
Other		
Other		

Peer Pressure

Think about the people in your life who pressure you to do things you do not want to do or try to stop you from doing what you want to do. In the spaces that follow, identify the people who pressure you and what they pressure you to do or not do.
(use name codes)

People Who Pressure Me	What They Pressure Me to Do or Not Do	How I Can Resist Being Pressured
Example: JUF	*Have a party at my house when there are no adults at home.*	*Saying no, no matter how difficult it will be for me.*

Peer Pressure Quotation

The creative individual has the capacity to free himself from the web of social pressures in which the rest of us are caught. He or she is capable of questioning the assumptions that the rest of us accept. ~ **John W. Gardner**

What is the author of the quote saying?

_____
_____
_____
_____
_____
_____
_____

How does the quote relate to a situation in your life?

_____
_____
_____
_____
_____
_____
_____

Why is this quote important?

_____
_____
_____
_____
_____
_____
_____

Peer Pressure Can Go Either Way

How has peer pressure affected you in a negative way?

_____
_____
_____
_____
_____
_____

How have I negatively influenced others?

_____
_____
_____
_____
_____
_____

Now, how has peer pressure affected you in a positive way?

_____
_____
_____
_____
_____

How have I positively influenced others?

_____
_____
_____
_____
_____
_____

Why Do Teens Give In to Peer Pressure?

- To avoid being bullied
- To avoid being made fun of or ridiculed
- To avoid being teased
- To avoid standing out as different
- To be accepted
- To be cool
- To be liked
- To be part of a crowd, social group, clique or gang
- To be popular
- To fit in because everyone else is doing it
- To not feel like an outcast
- To overcome or hide low self-esteem
- To try something new

Facts about Peer Pressure

- Peer pressure can be negative (used to coax you to engage in something you don't want to do.)
- Peer pressure can be positive (used to coax you to not hang out with hurtful people, to urge you to ask for help when needed).
- It is important to pay attention to your own feelings and beliefs about what is right.
- It is imperative for you to have friends who have similar values and beliefs as you.
- It is a MUST to firmly say *no* when you know something is wrong.

SECTION III:

Experiencing Dating Violence Scale

Name_____

Date_____

Experiencing Dating Violence Scale
Directions

Many teens find themselves in a dating relationship in which they are victims of violence. In many teen dating relationships, one partner tries to maintain power and control over the other through violence and abuse.

This assessment is designed to help you evaluate the attitudes of people whom you are considering dating.

This scale contains 28 statements that are divided into four specific violent attitudes. Read each statement and decide the extent to which the statement describes you.

Circle 3 if the statement is **a Lot like Him/Her**

Circle 2 if the statement is **a Little like Him/Her**

Circle 1 if the statement is **Not like Him/Her**

One person I am dating is ____ (name code)

This person is jealous of my relationships with other people. 3   (2)   1

In the above statement, the circled 2 means that the statement is a little like the person whom the test taker is dating. Ignore the TOTAL lines below each section. They are for scoring purposes and will be used later.

(Turn to the next page and begin)

Experiencing Dating Violence Scale

3 = A Lot Like Him/Her   2 = A Little Like Him/Her   1 = Not Like Him/Her

One person I am dating is _____ (use name code)

This person is jealous of my relationships with other people.	3	2	1
This person calls or texts me continually.	3	2	1
This person doesn't want me to spend time with my friends.	3	2	1
This person controls my social networks.	3	2	1
This person reads my e-mails and texts.	3	2	1
This person pressures me for an exclusive commitment.	3	2	1
This person accuses my friends and/or family of being against our relationship.	3	2	1

SECTION I TOTAL = _____

3 = A Lot Like Him/Her   2 = A Little Like Him/Her   1 = Not Like Him/Her

This person tries to control me.	3	2	1
This person does not want me to phone or text others.	3	2	1
This person does not like me to go places with others.	3	2	1
This person questions where I am a lot of the time.	3	2	1
This person wants to know about the people I talk to.	3	2	1
This person makes me ask for permission to do things I want to do.	3	2	1
This person isolates me from others.	3	2	1

SECTION II TOTAL = _____

(Continued on the next page)

Experiencing Dating Violence Scale *(Continued)*

3 = A Lot Like Him/Her   2 = A Little Like Him/Her   1 = Not Like Him/Her

This person was abused in the past.	3	2	1
This person abuses alcohol and/or drugs.	3	2	1
This person lies.	3	2	1
This person can be preoccupied with weapons.	3	2	1
This person has been in other abusive dating relationships.	3	2	1
This person is not trustworthy.	3	2	1
This person feels he or she is never wrong.	3	2	1

SECTION III TOTAL = _____

3 = A Lot Like Him/Her   2 = A Little Like Him/Her   1 = Not Like Him/Her

This person gets upset very easily.	3	2	1
This person is aggressive with others outside our relationship.	3	2	1
This person has unpredictable mood swings.	3	2	1
This person can be cruel.	3	2	1
This person criticizes me a lot.	3	2	1
This person abuses me physically, psychologically, verbally, emotionally, sexually and/or financially.	3	2	1
This person lives a high-risk lifestyle.	3	2	1

SECTION IV TOTAL = _____

(Go to the Scoring Directions on the next page)

Experiencing Dating Violence Scale
Scoring Directions

The Experiencing Dating Violence Scale is designed to help you determine if you are in a healthy relationship or in an abusive relationship. Add the numbers you've circled for each of the four sections on the previous pages. Put that total on the line marked TOTAL at the end of each section.

Then, transfer your totals for each of the four sections to the lines below:

SECTION I · **TOTAL** = _____ Jealousy

SECTION II · **TOTAL** = _____ Control

SECTION III · **TOTAL** = _____ Lifestyle

SECTION IV · **TOTAL** = _____ Abusiveness

GRAND TOTAL = _____

Profile Interpretation

Total Individual Scale Scores	Grand Total of all Four Scale Scores	Result	Indications
17 to 21	66 to 84	High	The person you are dating seems to have controlling and abusive tendencies.
12 to 16	46 to 65	Moderate	The person you are dating seems to have some signs of controlling and abusive tendencies.
7 to 11	28 to 45	Low	The person you are dating seems to have very few of the signs of having controlling and abusive tendencies, but this could still indicate some abusive behavior. Continue to do the following exercises.

For scales which you scored in the **Moderate** or **High** range, find the descriptions on the pages that follow. Read the description and complete the exercises that are included. No matter how you scored, low, moderate or high, you will benefit from these exercises. Self-advocacy strategies are included to ensure safe, healthy relationships for you.

Jealousy

Abusive boyfriends and girlfriends tend to be very possessive and controlling.

A possessive, controlling partner is jealous of relationships with outsiders, even family members. The abusive one may insist that their partner quit other activities that do not include him or her and may even demand that the partner provide detailed accounts of whereabouts and times when they are not together. The controller may want the partner to check in and/or may call several times a day to verify whereabouts. A frequent question is "Where were you?" The controller wants to do everything together, exclusive of others, and may want the partner to reduce or cut out altogether any time spent with family or other friends, isolating the partner.

At first, all of this personal attention may seem flattering, but it is not healthy!

How does your boyfriend or girlfriend show jealousy? (use name code)

_____

_____

_____

_____

What activities has this person asked you to quit and did you quit?

_____

_____

_____

_____

How did it feel doing that activity? If you quit, how did it feel to quit it?

_____

_____

_____

_____

How does this person keep track of your whereabouts? How does that feel to you?

_____

_____

_____

_____

Control

Abusive boyfriends and girlfriends attempt to impose their opinions on their partners. The controller may expect the partner to meet every demand, wish and need. The controller attempts to control their partner because they feel like the partner belongs to them and they want to control how and with whom the partner spends time. The controller may not want the partner to finish school because that would increase the partner's dependence on them. They may even require their partners to ask permission to do the things they want to do.

How does your boyfriend or girlfriend try to control you? (use name code)

_____

_____

_____

_____

What are your expectations of males and females in relationships?

_____

_____

_____

_____

Does this person meet those expectations?

_____

_____

_____

_____

In what ways does this person expect you to meet his or her wishes?

_____

_____

_____

_____

Lifestyle

Abusive boyfriends and girlfriends show their abusive behavior through the lifestyle they live. They tend to lie about their activities and their whereabouts, keeping parts of their life secret. They possibly use alcohol and/or illegal substances. They often have been abused in the past. They may be preoccupied with various types of weapons or explosives or other dangerous behaviors.

How does the lifestyle of your boyfriend or girlfriend concern you? (use name code)

_____

_____

_____

_____

_____

_____

_____

What do you know about this person's past relationships?

_____

_____

_____

_____

_____

_____

_____

What do you know about the person's past?

_____

_____

_____

_____

_____

_____

_____

Abusive Behavior

Abusive boyfriends or girlfriends tend to be abusive to their partners and to others. They tend to be explosive and display bad temper outbursts. They often show physical aggressiveness with other people they have dated. They are often verbally abusive to other people and blame others for their own mistakes or problems. They may be bullies in school. They can be very cruel to people and pets. They are extremely critical of other people.

How does the behavior of your boyfriend or girlfriend frighten you? (use name code)

_____

_____

_____

_____

_____

_____

_____

When has this person displayed a bad temper? Describe the situation.

_____

_____

_____

_____

_____

_____

_____

When has this person displayed physical aggressiveness? Describe the situation.

_____

_____

_____

_____

_____

_____

_____

Teen Dating Safety

Whether officially going on a date or simply going out with a group of friends, your parents, family, a good friend or trusted adult needs to know where you are going and with whom. Think about the next time you are going out and complete the following questions related to it. (use name codes)

Who will you be with?	
Who is responsible for transportation?	
Where will you be?	
What will you be doing?	
When will you be home?	
How will you contact your parents, etc., if you need to do so?	
What if your plans change?	
What do you need to be on guard against?	
Any other safety considerations?	

Self-Advocacy

Self-advocacy allows you to take control of your life and to take charge of your well-being and safety in future relationships. The following exercises will help you to be in control and take charge of your life.

Putting Yourself First

Self-advocates are able to put themselves first and get their wants and needs met without being selfish or ignoring others wants and needs.

How can you begin to put yourself first?

_____

_____

_____

What needs and wants do you have that you rarely, if ever, tell people?

_____

_____

_____

Who would you like to tell?

_____

_____

_____

Stand Up for Yourself

Self-advocates are able to stand up for themselves.

How can you begin to stand up for your rights?

_____

_____

_____

What decisions do you need to make based on what is in your best interest?

_____

_____

_____

Self-Advocacy

Dealing with the Negatives

Self-advocates are able to deal with negative or disrespectful comments.

What negative things have people said about or to you that are not true? Write about how they are not true.

_____

_____

_____

How do you tear yourself down with negative self-talk? Write about the things you say to yourself about yourself.

_____

_____

_____

Now write about you and give yourself the respect you deserve. What positive things do you deserve?

_____

_____

_____

Feeling Helpless

Self-advocates are able to be in control. List the times and ways you have been helpless and out of control in your relationships.

_____

_____

_____

Now list what you need to do to be less helpless and have more control over your life – doing what YOU want to do, without being selfish - not what your boyfriend or girlfriend wants you to do.

_____

_____

_____

Healthy Relationships

Many people find it difficult to develop and keep positive, healthy relationships. Look for relationships with people who will support you and treat you well. They may be your fellow students, co-workers, friends, siblings, parents, boyfriends, girlfriends or other family members. In the spaces below, describe the people with whom you have healthy relationships.

Person (use name code)	Relationship to Me	Reasons I Feel These Are Healthy Relationships

Changing Unhealthy Relationships

Many people find themselves in negative, unhealthy relationships. You might have such people around you; people who do not support you and do not treat you well. You have choices about how you will deal with people with whom you have unhealthy relationships. These choices will depend on your relationship with each individual and the reasons for the unhealthy relationship. People who are in physically abusive relationships, or ones with a threat of physical abuse, need a plan in place. Complete the page below. (use name codes)

Person (name code)	Relationship to Me	Reasons I Feel these Are Unhealthy Relationships	Actions I Will Take and When

Trusting Relationships

Write about the people you know who have great relationships. List what you have observed about their behaviors towards each other. (use name codes)

Family

_____
_____
_____
_____
_____

Friends

_____
_____
_____
_____
_____

Acquaintances / Neighbors

_____
_____
_____
_____
_____

Co-workers / Volunteer-workers

_____
_____
_____
_____
_____

Others

_____
_____
_____
_____
_____

Dating Safety

When dating, keep some of these tips in mind:

- Consider double-dating the first time you go out with a new person. Whom could you ask to double-date?

- If you are going alone, do not drive with a new person whom you do not know well. Meet the person somewhere and have your own transportation or ride.

- If stranded, have contact people you could call for a ride. Who are those people?

- Make sure a family member or a trusted adult or friend know your plans and what time you are expected home.

- Meeting in a public place during daylight hours is advisable on a first date.

- Don't accept rides from people you do not know well. Ask for a ride from your parents or contact people. If you must leave a party or event with a person whom you do not know well, let a parent or a trusted person know the driver's identity and your plans, and ask the person to call, to make sure you arrive home safely.

- Be assertive when you need to be. Be honest, firm, and straightforward in your dating relationships.

- If you begin to feel uncomfortable, find a safe way to remove yourself from the situation.

- Do not use any substances that could impair your judgment or go anywhere, particularly in a vehicle or on a motorcycle, with someone who has been using judgment-impairing substances.

- Guard any drink you might have to be sure no one slips any drugs or any other harmful substances into the drink. Guard your personal belongings as well.

- Being able to contact others is important - and a cell phone is helpful for this. Leave or relate a general plan of your itinerary and call if it changes.

Is anyone willing to share an experience that happened to them, or to someone they know? Please do not use names.

Warning Signs of an Abusive Dating Relationship

The following is a checklist of potential early warning signs of an abusive dating partner. What is the name code of a person you are dating? _____

Check off the items below that seem to be an indication of this person's personality.

❑ Is jealous

❑ Demonstrates a controlling, demanding behavior

❑ Shows unpredictable mood swings

❑ Has an explosive temper when angry

❑ Uses illegal substances and alcohol

❑ Isolates me from others

❑ Is verbally abusive

❑ Is financially abusive

❑ Is psychologically abusive

❑ Is sexually abusive

❑ Is physically abusive

❑ Is emotionally abusive

❑ Blames others for his/her problems

❑ Threatens violence

❑ Checks in with me too often

❑ Constantly fighting

❑ Constantly instigating fights

❑ Pressures me to do things I don't want to do

❑ Is becoming too serious too fast

❑ Uses weapons in a threatening or destructive way

❑ Blames me for negative things that happen

❑ Believes in stereotypical gender roles for men and women

Assertive Communication

To communicate effectively...

- Own your messages by beginning with *"I..."*

- Be confident about yourself and your abilities.

- Choose the right time and place, not when you're upset.

- Have a clear idea of what you want to say. Be specific.

- Avoid bringing up the past – stay in the here and now.

- Pay attention to your feelings and express them honestly.

- Focus on behaviors. *"I get scared when you leave me alone at wild parties."*

- Have a relaxed posture.

- Use positive body language – no hands on hips or finger pointing.

- Stand up for your rights.

- Respect the rights of others.

- Use a clear, calm tone of voice.

- Listen without interrupting.

- Consider the other person's point of view.

- Maintain personal space boundaries.

- Respond to criticism in an open and direct way without raising your voice or appearing angry.

- State what you want. *"I would prefer not to go if you are not going to stay with me."*

SECTION IV:

Potential for Violence? Scale

Name_____

Date_____

Potential for Violence? Scale
Directions

Many teens become violent in their dating relationships without being aware of their own behavior. In your teen dating relationships, you may try to maintain power and control over others through violence and abuse.

This assessment is designed to help you think about whether you have a violent attitude or behavior with the people you date.

This scale contains 28 statements that are divided into four specific violence categories. Read each statement and decide the extent to which the statement describes you.

Circle 3 if the statement is **a Lot like me**

Circle 2 if the statement is **a Little like me**

Circle 1 if the statement is **Not like me**

One person I am having a relationship with is _____ (name code)

In this relationship ...

I am jealous of this person's relationships with others 3   (2)   1

In the above statement, the circled 2 means that the statement is a little like the person whom the test taker is dating. Ignore the TOTAL lines below each section. They are for scoring purposes and will be used later.

(Turn to the next page and begin)

Potential for Violence? Scale

3 = A Lot Like Me **2 = A Little Like Me** **1 = Not Like Me**

One person I am having a relationship with is _____ (name code)

In this relationship . . .

I am jealous of this person's relationships with others	3	2	1
I call or text this person constantly	3	2	1
I resent this person spending time with anyone else.	3	2	1
I control what this person writes on social networks.	3	2	1
I read this person's e-mails and texts.	3	2	1
I pressure this person for an exclusive commitment	3	2	1
I accuse this person's friends and family of causing trouble in our relationship	3	2	1

SECTION I TOTAL = _____

3 = A Lot Like Me **2 = A Little Like Me** **1 = Not Like Me**

In this relationship . . .

I try to control this person	3	2	1
I do not want this person to phone or text anyone else	3	2	1
I do not approve of this person going anywhere without me	3	2	1
I question where this person is most of the time.	3	2	1
I want to know about anyone this person talks to.	3	2	1
I insist that this person asks for permission to do anything	3	2	1
I am very possessive when it comes to this person.	3	2	1

SECTION II TOTAL = _____

(Continued on the next page)

Potential for Violence? Scale *(Continued)*

3 = A Lot Like Me   2 = A Little Like Me   1 = Not Like Me

Honestly, about me:

I was abused in the past 3   2   1

I abuse alcohol and/or drugs 3   2   1

I lie some of the time 3   2   1

I am very interested in weapons and explosives 3   2   1

I have abused someone in a dating relationship 3   2   1

I have a history of being untrustworthy in the past 3   2   1

I rarely say "I'm sorry" for anything that happens 3   2   1

SECTION III TOTAL = _____

3 = A Lot Like Me   2 = A Little Like Me   1 = Not Like Me

Honestly, about me:

I get upset very easily 3   2   1

I am aggressive with others outside our relationship 3   2   1

I have unpredictable mood swings 3   2   1

I can be cruel 3   2   1

I criticize people a lot 3   2   1

I physically, emotionally and/or verbally abuse this person 3   2   1

I live a high-risk lifestyle 3   2   1

SECTION IV TOTAL = _____

(Go to the Scoring Directions on the next page)

Potential for Violence? Scale
Scoring Directions

The Potential for Violence? Scale is designed to help you determine if you are potentially abusive in your dating relationships. Add the numbers you've circled for each of the four sections on the previous pages. Put that total on the line marked TOTAL at the end of each section.

Then, transfer your totals for each of the four sections to the lines below:

SECTION I	- TOTAL	=	_____	**Jealousy**
SECTION II	- TOTAL	=	_____	**Control**
SECTION III	- TOTAL	=	_____	**Lifestyle**
SECTION IV	- TOTAL	=	_____	**Abusive behavior**

GRAND TOTAL = _____

Profile Interpretation

Total Individual Scale Scores	Grand Total Scale Scores	Result	Indications
17 to 21	67 to 84	High	You show many controlling and abusive tendencies.
12 to 16	46 to 66	Moderate	You show quite a few signs of having controlling and abusive tendencies.
7 to 11	28 to 45	Low	You show very few of the signs of having controlling and abusive tendencies but, depending on your responses, this could still indicate abusive behavior.

For scales which you scored in the **Moderate** or **High** range, find the descriptions on the pages that follow. Read the description and complete the exercises that are included. No matter how you scored, low, moderate or high, you will benefit from these exercises. Self-advocacy strategies are included to ensure safe, healthy relationships for you.

Jealousy

Abusive boyfriends and girlfriends tend to be very possessive and controlling. A possessive, controlling partner is jealous of relationships with outsiders, even family members. The abusive one may insist that their partner quit other activities that do not include him or her and may even demand that the partner provide detailed accounts of whereabouts and times when they are not together. The controller may want the partner to check in and/or may call several times a day to verify whereabouts. A frequent question is "Where were you?" The controller wants to do everything together, exclusive of others, and may want the partner to reduce or cut out altogether any time spent with family or other friends, isolating the partner. At first all of this personal attention may seem flattering to their partner, but their partner will eventually realize that this is not healthy!

How do you show your jealousy in your dating relationships? (use name codes)

_____

_____

_____

_____

_____

_____

What activities have you asked dating partners to quit? What reasons did you give?

_____

_____

_____

_____

_____

How do you keep track of your dating partners' whereabouts?

_____

_____

_____

_____

_____

Control

Abusive boyfriends and girlfriends attempt to impose their opinions on their partners. The controller may expect the partner to meet every demand, wish and need. The controller attempts to control their partner because they feel like the partner belongs to them and they want to control how and with whom the partner spends time. The controller may not want the partner to finish school because that would increase the partner's dependence on them. They may even require their partners to ask permission to do the things they want to do.

How do you try to control others you date? (use name codes)

_____

_____

_____

_____

_____

_____

What is your view of the roles of males and females in relationships?

_____

_____

_____

_____

_____

_____

In what ways do you expect people you date to meet your wishes?

_____

_____

_____

_____

_____

_____

Lifestyle

Abusive boyfriends and girlfriends show their abusive behavior through the lifestyle they live. They tend to lie about their activities and their whereabouts, keeping parts of their life secret. They possibly use alcohol and/or illegal substances. They often have been abused in the past. They may be preoccupied with various types of weapons or explosives or other dangerous behaviors.

Describe how your lifestyle might concern the person in your dating relationship. (use name codes)

_____

_____

_____

_____

_____

_____

What should your dating partners know about your past relationships?

_____

_____

_____

_____

_____

_____

Even if you don't want them to know, what should your dating partners know about your past?

_____

_____

_____

_____

_____

_____

Abusive Behavior

Abusive boyfriends or girlfriends tend to be abusive to their partners and to others. They tend to be explosive and display bad temper outbursts. They often show physical aggressiveness with other people they have dated. They are often verbally abusive to other people and blame others for their own mistakes or problems. They may be bullies in school. They can be very cruel to people and pets. They are extremely critical of other people.

Describe how your behavior might concern or scare a person you are dating. (use name codes)

_____

_____

_____

_____

_____

_____

List the times and situations where you have shown a bad temper.

_____

_____

_____

_____

_____

_____

List the times and situations where you have shown physical aggressiveness.

_____

_____

_____

_____

_____

_____

Managing Violent Behavior

It is important for you to learn how to manage your angry, violent behavior. Following are some general techniques that can help you manage your attitude and behavior:

STEP 1: Understand Your Bodily Reactions

It will be helpful to begin by paying attention to the signals being sent by your body so that you can identify when you are beginning to feel your anger that eventually leads to violence. Explore what you are experiencing and become attuned to the physical sensations surging through your body. The first step in managing your anger is reading the signals your body is sending to you as you begin to feel angry. (use name codes)

Think about the last time you got angry. What prompted the anger?

_____

_____

_____

_____

How did your body signal you when you were getting angry?

_____

_____

_____

_____

How did your body feel?

_____

_____

_____

_____

How different did you feel when the anger had passed?

_____

_____

_____

STEP 2: Learn to Calm Your Body

Become adept at calming your bodily reaction to anger. Relax your body by taking a time-out from the situation; focus on something else; focus on breathing deeply; engage in activities that will reduce the tension associated with feelings of anger and tension in your body. The second step in managing your anger is now to begin to calm your body using relaxation techniques. (use name codes)

What techniques can you use to calm your body when you are angry?

_____

_____

_____

_____

_____

_____

_____

How does this help your body return to normal?

_____

_____

_____

_____

_____

_____

_____

What have you tried that has not worked for you? What has worked?

_____

_____

_____

_____

_____

_____

_____

_____

STEP 3: Redirect Your Mind

Look at any angry situation with logic, reason and clarity. By thinking in a calm and rational way, you can gain control of your behavior and respond in a way that is not explosive toward other people. Eliminate negative self-talk that is going on in your own mind. Redirect those negative thoughts. (use name codes)

Here's an example:

In an angry situation this negative thought might have come into your head:

I'm going get even with MCW after school.

How could you have redirected that thought?

MCW might have been having a tough day. – OR – Fighting will get us both in trouble. – OR – I'll talk to MCW later, when I'm not so angry.

What is an angry situation you were involved in recently?

_____

_____

_____

_____

_____

What negative thoughts kept coming into your head?

_____

_____

_____

_____

_____

How could you have redirected your thoughts?

_____

_____

_____

_____

_____

STEP 4: Communicate Assertively

It is vital to communicate effectively with others even when you are angry. Control your body posture, gestures, volume and tone of voice to communicate assertively to others in the situation. Respond openly, honestly and directly, in a non-threatening and non-confrontational manner, to make your point. The last step in the anger management process is to assertively communicate your feelings and needs to others around you. (use name codes)

Here's an example:

How did you communicate in your angry situation?

I yelled at MHJ, "You've got to be kidding!" and walked away.

How would it be different if you were not angry?

I probably would explain to MHJ why I would never cheat.

What is an angry situation you were involved in recently?

_____

_____

_____

_____

How did you communicate in that situation?

_____

_____

_____

_____

How could it have been different if you had waited until you were not so angry?

_____

_____

_____

_____

What communication skills do you need to work on?

_____

_____

_____

_____

Dating Situations that Push My Buttons

Often there are annoying and anger-producing dating situations that seem to push hot buttons. Below, list the situations in which you get angry and explain why you seem to get so angry. (use name codes)

Situations in which I Get Angry	Why I Become Angry and How I Can Address My Anger
Ex: Lateness	LJT is always late. It makes me angry because I am always on time and because he is not considerate of me. I will calmly, yet assertively, make him aware of why I become angry when he is late.

My Dating Anger Log

Anger reactions are composed of a series of learned behaviors and choices. The following anger log will help you to keep track of your thoughts, feelings, and behaviors related to your anger on dates. Think back to a time when you were angry on a date and complete the following log. (use name codes)

Photocopy this dating anger log to continue to track your anger in the future.

Describe what was happening when you got angry.

_____

_____

_____

How did your body change?

_____

_____

_____

How did you try to calm your body?

_____

_____

_____

What thoughts triggered the anger?

_____

_____

_____

How did you redirect your thinking?

_____

_____

_____

How did you communicate to resolve the problem?

_____

_____

_____

Dating Pet Peeves

Write about the types of things that anger you when you are on a date.

_____

_____

_____

_____

_____

_____

_____

_____

_____

_____

_____

_____

An Ideal Relationship

How would you describe an "ideal" intimate and trusting relationship?

_____

_____

_____

_____

_____

_____

_____

_____

_____

_____

_____

_____

Ways to Cope with Anger

- Be aware of what you're feeling and thinking
- Breathe deeply
- Come back and talk it out calmly and reasonably
- Count 10 breaths
- Dance
- Distract yourself
- Exercise
- Express your feelings in "I-Statements"
- Journal – Write about your thoughts and feelings
- Know the difference between feeling anger or just feeling annoyed or inconvenienced
- Know what triggers your anger and avoid those situations
- Listen to calming music
- Plan time wisely so you're not hassled and easily angered
- Play a musical instrument
- Recognize your warning signs of anger
- Sing a favorite song
- Take a walk outside
- Talk with a trusted friend or trusted adult
- Think before reacting
- Walk away
- Use your self-control – YOU CAN DO IT!

Symptoms of Anger

All people have symptoms of anger that tell them that they are feeling angry.

Physical Signs

Clenched fists

Clenched jaws

Fast breathing

Fast heartbeat

Frowning, scowling

Headaches

Red face

Stomach pains

Shaking

Sweating

Tense muscles

Tight chest

Upset feeling in the stomach

Psychological Signs

Angry thoughts

Confusion

Irritability

Memory problems

Obsess about issues

Problems concentrating

Short-tempered

Thoughts of doing harm

Behavioral Signs

Pacing

Swearing

Throwing things

Withdrawing from others

Yelling

SECTION V:

Personal Safety Scale

Name_____

Date_____

Personal Safety Scale
Directions

For teens, staying safe can be difficult. Whether it is in the home, school, work place, community, social media, or on a date, teens often find their safety is at risk.

This scale can help you identify how safe you are in the various aspects of your life. It contains 25 statements. Read each of the statements and decide how much the statement applies to you. In each of the choices listed, circle the response on the right of each statement.

In the following example, the circled 2 indicates that the person completing the assessment is sometimes aware of surroundings.

	Often	**Sometimes**	**Never**
I am aware of my surroundings when I go out	3	(2)	1

This is not a test. Since there are no right or wrong answers, do not spend too much time thinking about your answers. Be sure to respond to every statement.

(Turn to the next page and begin)

Personal Safety Scale

	Often	Sometimes	Never
I am aware of my surroundings when I go out	3	2	1
I don't walk alone in unfamiliar places	3	2	1
I stay away from isolated areas	3	2	1
I avoid dark areas	3	2	1
I carry my cell phone with me at all times	3	2	1
I keep in touch with people I trust to tell them where I am	3	2	1
I don't let others pressure me to do things I don't want to do	3	2	1
I keep the doors and windows locked at home when I'm alone	3	2	1
I will leave an uncomfortable situation	3	2	1
I spend my time with people who make me feel safe	3	2	1
I have trusted family and friends to talk to about violence	3	2	1
I set all of my online profiles to be private	3	2	1
I tell trusted others when I am experiencing any form of abuse	3	2	1
I give my passwords only to a trusted member of my family	3	2	1
I do not answer calls from blocked numbers or any number I do not recognize	3	2	1
I block phone numbers of people I don't want to talk with	3	2	1
I never give out personal information	3	2	1
I never personally meet with anyone I have met online	3	2	1
I don't surf the Internet in places that are not appropriate or safe	3	2	1
I am careful about whom I date	3	2	1
I have a safety plan for leaving a situation if I need to	3	2	1
I can be assertive when I need to be	3	2	1
I won't do anything online that I wouldn't do in person	3	2	1
I choose my friends carefully	3	2	1
I do not give in to peer pressure	3	2	1

(Go to the Scoring Directions on the next page)

Personal Safety Scale
Scoring Directions

In this often violent world, personal safety should always be in your mind, regardless of the situation. This assessment is designed to help you identify your level of personal safety with a variety of situations.

To score the assessment:

Add the number of the responses you circled on the assessment. Then, transfer your total to the line below:

Personal Safety Total = _____

Profile Interpretation

Total Scales Scores	Result	Indications
Scores from 59 to 75	high	You are taking precautions to be safe. The following sections will help you develop a more comprehensive personal safety plan.
Scores from 42 to 58	moderate	You are taking some precautions to be safe. The following sections will help you develop a personal safety plan.
Scores from 25 to 41	low	You are taking very few precautions to be safe. The following sections will help you develop a personal safety plan.

For scales which you scored in the **Moderate** or **High** range, find the descriptions on the pages that follow. Then, read the description and complete the exercises that are included. No matter how you scored, low, moderate or high, you will benefit from these exercises.

Feeling Safe

School, Home, Dating Relationships, Work, Volunteer Place, Community, Social Media ... Anywhere

When or where do you feel safe?

1._____

2._____

3. _____

With whom do you feel safe? (use name codes)

1._____

2._____

3. _____

When or where do you not feel safe?

1._____

2._____

3. _____

With whom do you not feel safe? (use name codes)

1._____

2._____

3. _____

Safety at Home

Be aware of the following to ensure your safety at home:

- If you do not feel safe, try not to be alone with that person.
- If you are home alone, make sure doors are locked and windows are secure.
- Check to see if windows and doors have locks and are in good repair.
- Never open the door to someone you don't know.
- Do not let strangers use your phone.
- Do not tell unknown callers that you are, or going to be, alone in the house.
- Do not put on social media that you are, or going to be, alone in the house.
- Don't give out personal information over the phone or your computer.
- If you are concerned about being home alone, speak with a trusted adult.
- At all times have access to emergency call numbers.

My Home Safety Plan

What can you do to prevent or eliminate violence you might experience at home?
(use name codes)

Situation	What I will do	How I will feel safer
Example: Stranger coming to the door and asking to come in because of an emergency need to use the phone.	*Not respond nor open the door.*	*Tell myself that if it is valid, this person can go to someone else's house to get help. Call the police if the person is persistent.*

Safety at School

Be aware of the following to ensure your safety in school:

- Commit to receiving the best education possible.
- Develop friends who have similar classes, interests and values as you.
- Become involved in school activities.
- Avoid high-risk, unsupervised activities or areas.
- Be aware of, and avoid, gang activity.
- Be aware of bullying.
- Do not be a bystander to bullying.
- In a confidential way, report bullying or violent acts to school administrators or teachers.
- Learn how to interact with peers and pick up on cues.
- Use a buddy system with one friend or a group of friends.
- Never have, or be with anyone who has, a weapon or explosive.
- Develop a relationship with a trusted adult who can serve as an ally for me.

My School Safety Plan

What can you do to prevent or eliminate violence you might experience at school?
(use name codes)

Situation	What I will do	How I will feel safer
Example: A bully is cornering you on your way to your first class.	*Begin walking to school with LBH who is also in the class.*	*Bullies tend to isolate the people they pick on.*

Safety at Work and Volunteering

Be aware of the following to ensure your safety at work or volunteer place:

- Be aware that bullying happens in the work and volunteer place also.
- Deal confidently and assertively with bullies.
- Do not be a bystander to bullying.
- Try not to work alone where you can be victimized.
- Be aware of safety procedures.
- Know the instructions for reporting bullying or violence.
- Know the right person to report bullying or violence.
- Be assertive when being verbally abused.
- Learn how to interact with co-workers and pick up on cues.
- Beware of supervisors who try to intimidate you or act inappropriately.
- If needed, use a buddy system with one co-worker or a group of co-workers.
- Confide in a trusted adult.
- Never have, or be with anyone who has, a weapon or explosive.
- Report any harassment to a supervisor.

My Work and/or Volunteer Place Safety Plan

What can you do to prevent or eliminate violence you might experience at work or your volunteer place? (use name codes)

Situation	What I will do	How I will feel safer
Example: A co-worker is verbally abusing me at work.	I will let my boss know what is happening, and then I will stand up to the person.	I will know that I can be assertive when I need to be.

Safety with Dating Relationships

Be aware of the following to ensure your safety with a person you are dating:

- Go out with a group of friends, or double date for your first date.
- Do not be alone in a car until you feel very safe.
- Make sure others know where you are on your date.
- Be aware of the probability that you will be unable to react effectively while using any illegal substances.
- Carry your cell phone fully charged.
- Let your date know that you are expected to call in at a certain time.
- Remove yourself from the situation if you feel uncomfortable.
- If you are even a little suspicious, trust your instincts.
- Do not even consider another date with this person if he or she is abusive in any way.
- Learn how pick up on cues.
- Never have, or be with anyone who has, a weapon or explosive.

My Dating Safety Plan

What can you do to prevent or eliminate violence with a date? (use name codes)

Situation	What I will do	How I will feel safer
Example: I have had bad experiences on first dates in the past.	*I will ask my friend JSC and her boyfriend if they want to double-date this first date.*	*I will have people I trust with me if the date does not go well.*

Safety within My Community

Be aware of the following to ensure your safety within your community:

- Consider going out with a group of friends.
- Avoid dark places.
- Be aware of your surroundings.
- Don't walk alone.
- Carry your cell phone fully charged.
- Try not to be alone in a car until you feel very safe.
- Avoid individuals who have a history of aggressive behavior, limited social skills, or demonstrate a violent attitude.
- Remove yourself from the situation if you feel uncomfortable.
- If you are even a little suspicious, trust your instincts.
- Learn how pick up on cues.
- Never have, or be with anyone who has, a weapon or explosive.

My Safety Plan within My Community

What can you do to prevent or eliminate violence within your community? (use name codes)

Situation	What I will do	How I will feel safer
Example: I usually jog on a somewhat isolated road around my neighborhood.	*I will begin jogging in the park where there are more people around.*	*I will feel safer being around other people.*

Safety with Social Media

Be aware of the following to ensure your safety with social media:

- Never give out personal information online.
- Never give out privacy compromising photographs online.
- Do not agree online to meet with someone you do not know.
- Block bullying or combative online users.
- Beware of cyber-bullying. Don't allow others to be abusive to you online.
- Don't give your phone number to anyone unless you know them personally.
- Do not enter contests or join clubs where you need to give ANY personal information. (phone number, city, state, email, parents name, etc,)
- If you are even a little suspicious, trust your instincts.
- Learn how pick up on cues.
- If a strange person contacts you through chat rooms, emails or texts, tell a trusted adult. Do not respond.
- Being online is the same as being in public. It may feel safe and secure but there are huge privacy issues. Protect yourself.
- Remember that privacy settings are not reliable or trustworthy.

My Safety Plan with Social Media

What can you do to prevent or eliminate abuse or violence with social media? (use name codes)

Situation	What I will do	How I will feel safer
Example: I met KZ from my social networking site. It was not a good experience!	I won't ever again meet with people I only know from social networking sites.	I will not have to worry about meeting with people who might harm me.

Feeling Safe ... or NOT?

In what areas of your life (home, school, work, volunteer-place, dating, community or social media) do you feel the safest and why?

_____

_____

_____

_____

_____

_____

_____

_____

_____

In what areas of your life do you not feel very safe and why?

_____

_____

_____

_____

_____

_____

_____

_____

_____

What can you do about it?
(If you do not know, talk with a school counselor or another trusted adult.)

_____

_____

_____

_____

_____

_____

_____

_____

A Magazine Article

If you, yourself, or any person that you know, had an experience with a safety issue, write a short story about it and use a fictitious name. If you don't know anyone that has had this experience, write a fictional story about someone that did.

Make it so creative and interesting that a magazine would want to print it!

Title: _____

Story: _____

_____

_____

_____

_____

_____

_____

_____

_____

_____

_____

_____

_____

_____

_____

_____

_____

_____

_____

_____

_____

_____

_____

_____

Personal Safety while Driving

- Always park in areas that are well lit.

- Be sure you have enough fuel to get you to your destination and back, without having to stop in unknown areas.

- Have your keys out and ready to use as you approach your car.

- Before getting into the car, look to make sure that nobody is already inside the car or lurking around outside.

- Lock your doors as quickly as possible.

- Do not hitchhike or give rides to hitchhikers.

- If someone you know gives you a ride, ask them to wait until you enter your building.

- Do not give a ride to anyone you do NOT know.

General Safety Procedures

- Do not carry a weapon or explosives or be with anyone who has a weapon or explosives. Weapon availability only enhances violence.

- Report violent acts or threats of violence to the proper authorities or a trusted adult.

- Use effective conflict resolution skills to help others settle disputes before they turn into violent encounters.

- Refuse to give in to negative peer pressure.

- Choose your friends carefully. Have friends who share your interests and values.

- Be careful about spending time with people who show warning signs of violence.

- Talk to trusted adults for advice about handling violent situations.

100

SECTION VI:

Symptoms of Experiencing Violence Scale

Name_____

Date_____

Symptoms of Experiencing Violence Scale Directions

Like adults, teens go through the same types of reactions to violence. The Symptoms of Experiencing Violence Scale is designed to help you explore different types of symptoms that you may be experiencing. These symptoms are related to violent situations in your life.

This scale contains statements that are divided into five categories.
Read each of the statements and decide how descriptive the statement is of you.
In each of the choices listed, circle the number of your response on the line to the right of each statement.

In the following example, the circled 1 indicates the statement is not at all descriptive of the person completing the inventory:

	A Lot Like Me	Somewhat Like Me	A Little Like Me	Not Like Me
1.				
I feel detached from other people around me 4		3	2	(1)

This is not a test. Since there are no right or wrong answers, do not spend too much time thinking about your answers. Be sure to respond to every statement.

Think about a violent situation in which you recently found yourself. This situation may have involved you or a friend or a family member. What happened in the situation?

_____

_____

_____

Answer the questions based on this situation.

(Turn to the next page and begin)

Symptoms of Experiencing Violence Scale

Violence includes physical, psychological, emotional, verbal, sexual and financial abuse.

	A Lot Like Me	Somewhat Like Me	A Little Like Me	Not Like Me
I.				
I feel detached from other people around me	4	3	2	1
I have lost interest in important social activities	4	3	2	1
I have no interest in school	4	3	2	1
I don't care about my hobbies or my sports	4	3	2	1
I avoid activities or places that remind me of the violence	4	3	2	1
I avoid people or conversations that remind me of the violence	4	3	2	1
I have difficulty being around my friends	4	3	2	1
I try to avoid feelings that remind me of the violence	4	3	2	1

I - TOTAL = _____

	A Lot Like Me	Somewhat Like Me	A Little Like Me	Not Like Me
II.				
I have bad dreams or nightmares about the violence	4	3	2	1
I am jumpy if startled by sudden noises	4	3	2	1
I have difficulty falling asleep	4	3	2	1
I have a difficult time focusing and concentrating	4	3	2	1
I am on guard most of the time	4	3	2	1
I can feel my heart pounding rapidly	4	3	2	1
I find myself breathing rapidly when I think of the violence . . .	4	3	2	1
I have bruises on my body.	4	3	2	1

II - TOTAL = _____

(Continued on the next page)

Symptoms of Experiencing Violence Scale (Continued)

Violence includes physical, psychological, emotional, verbal, sexual and financial abuse.

	A Lot Like Me	Somewhat Like Me	A Little Like Me	Not Like Me
III.				
I think about the violence a lot of the time	4	3	2	1
I get mental pictures of the violence without being reminded of it	4	3	2	1
I am unable to make decisions.	4	3	2	1
I am unable to remember my life during the violence	4	3	2	1
I have sudden flashbacks of the violence.	4	3	2	1
I become upset because I think I should have done things differently.	4	3	2	1
I relive the violence in my mind.	4	3	2	1
I believe that I am not entitled to be happy	4	3	2	1
			III - TOTAL = _____	
IV.				
I feel numb emotionally	4	3	2	1
I feel guilty about the violence.	4	3	2	1
I become emotionally upset when I think about the violence	4	3	2	1
I am unable to experience love again	4	3	2	1
I become angry when I am reminded of the violence	4	3	2	1
I feel grief or sorrow when I think about the violence	4	3	2	1
I am irritable a lot of the time	4	3	2	1
I become angry very easily	4	3	2	1
			IV - TOTAL = _____	
V.				
I become depressed and then consider suicide	4	3	2	1
I self-medicate by consuming drugs or alcohol	4	3	2	1
I feel control over myself when I self-injure	4	3	2	1
I cut myself and/or belong to a cut club	4	3	2	1
I burn myself or break my bones.	4	3	2	1
I stop eating properly.	4	3	2	1
I engage in high-risk activities	4	3	2	1
I pull my hair or scratch myself	4	3	2	1
			V - TOTAL = _____	

(Go to the Scoring Directions on the next page)

Symptoms of Experiencing Violence Scale Scoring Directions

People who witness or are part of a violent event continue to experience stressful symptoms after the event. The Symptoms of Violence Scale is designed to measure the severity and the nature of the symptoms you are currently experiencing. For each of the five sections on the previous pages, count the scores you circled for each of the eight items. Put that total on the line marked "Total" at the end of each section.

Then, transfer your totals to the spaces below:

I.	**Detached Total**	=	_____
II.	**Physical Symptoms Total**	=	_____
III.	**Cognitive Total**	=	_____
IV.	**Emotions Total**	=	_____
V.	**Self-Destructive Behavior Total**	=	_____

Profile Interpretation

Individual Scales Scores	Result	Indications
Scores from 25 to 32	High	You have many of the symptoms of extreme stress. You need to find ways you can eliminate some of the stress in your life.
Scores from 16 to 24	Moderate	You have some of the symptoms of extreme stress. You need to find ways you can eliminate some of the stress in your life.
Scores from 8 to 15	Low	You may not have any, or you may have a few of the symptoms of extreme stress. It is always helpful to find ways to reduce the stress in your life.

For scales which you scored in the **Moderate** or **High** range, find the descriptions on the pages that follow. Read the description and complete the exercises that are included. No matter how you scored, low, moderate or high, you will benefit from these exercises.

Detached

People who are experiencing extreme stress are often detached and have lost interest in life. You possibly have lost interest in activities that are important to you like your job, school, hobbies, sports, house of worship or spiritual activities, and/or social activities. You may feel cut off and disconnected from people and have trouble being around friends and family.

Who are some of the people from whom you feel disconnected? (use name code)

_____

_____

_____

_____

_____

_____

List some of the things you have normally done that you no longer feel like doing.

_____

_____

_____

_____

_____

_____

How can you resume some of your activities, especially those you miss?

_____

_____

_____

_____

_____

_____

Physical Symptoms

People who are experiencing or have experienced violence usually experience extreme physical symptoms such as having trouble falling asleep, feeling irritable all of the time, having unusual aches and pains, feeling angry a lot of the time, and being hyper-alert or on-guard all of the time.

What physical symptoms do you experience most often?

_____

_____

_____

_____

_____

_____

_____

How are these physical symptoms affecting your life?

_____

_____

_____

_____

_____

_____

_____

What can you do and who can you talk with about the symptoms and the reason(s) you are experiencing them?

_____

_____

_____

_____

_____

_____

_____

Cognitive

People who are experiencing extreme stress often have symptoms that revolve around the recollection of the violence. These unwanted thoughts or images about the violence can occur while watching a certain television program, hearing a certain song, smelling a familiar fragrance, reading about something in the newspaper or can simply happen for no reason at all.

If this has happened in the past few months, describe the situation and what happened.

_____

_____

_____

_____

_____

_____

_____

What situations seem to bring the flashbacks on (television program, music, etc.)?

_____

_____

_____

_____

_____

How have you been coping with these thoughts?

_____

_____

_____

_____

_____

_____

Emotions

People who have been exposed to violence usually experience symptoms that include intense feelings such as anxiety, fear, grief, depression, guilt, anger and irritability. These feelings need to be dealt with and controlled for you to successfully move on with your life. These feelings can keep you from reducing or managing the stress in your life.

What feelings do you experience most intensely?

_____

_____

_____

_____

_____

What are the triggers for your feelings?

_____

_____

_____

_____

_____

How are you attempting to manage these strong emotions?

_____

_____

_____

_____

_____

_____

Self-Destructive Behavior

People who have been exposed to violence often experience symptoms that are self-destructive in nature. Self-destructive behavior is often the result of an inability to effectively handle or express feelings. It is often a way of controlling the body when people can't control anything else. Some people feel such emptiness that they feel pain is better than feeling nothing at all. Unfortunately, self-injury can be addictive if not stopped. These self-destructive behaviors negatively impact the body and mind and can lead to depression and possibly death.

What self-destructive behaviors do you engage in?

_____

_____

_____

_____

_____

_____

What triggers this behavior?

_____

_____

_____

_____

_____

_____

What feelings are you attempting to manage by engaging in self-destructive behaviors?

_____

_____

_____

_____

_____

_____

Exercises for Stress Reduction

Pick and choose the stress-reduction exercises that will work for you.

Staying in the Present

Much of the stress that you are experiencing comes from dwelling on the past or worrying about future events. To reduce and ultimately stop these thoughts, you need to start living in the present moment. When you do this, all of your attention becomes focused on what you are currently doing, and when this happens, all worries, fears and desires cease to enter your consciousness. As you begin to focus your attention, you will notice that thoughts of the past and future will arise. When they do, note it and gently turn your awareness back to the present.

Experiential Exercise – Staying in the Present

Try the following exercise to see how easy it is for you to relax. Sit still for several minutes and try to quiet your logical mind. Close your eyes and stop the internal chatter going on in your mind. Let go or block out any interfering thoughts, anxieties or emotions that pop into your head. Try not to think about the past or the future. Simply concentrate on your breath.

Exercise

Exercise is another excellent method for combating and managing stress and relieving some of the physical symptoms you may be experiencing. In our society, the time needed to exercise is often very hard to find, but it is very important that you put aside time each week in order to exercise your body and relieve tension. Several different types of exercises are available for you to use in reducing stress:

Aerobic exercise uses sustained, rhythmic activity involving primarily the large muscles in your legs. Aerobic exercises include such activities as jogging, running, brisk walking, swimming, bicycling, kickboxing or other high intensity martial arts and aerobic training. The goal of aerobic exercise is to gradually increase your stamina and enhance your cardiovascular system.

Low Intensity Exercise is used to increase muscle strength, enhance flexibility and quiet your mind. Low intensity exercises include slow walking, light gardening, yoga, walking in the woods, calisthenics and *soft* martial arts like Tai Chi.

Affirmations

When thoughts about past abuse begin to pop into your head, one of the best tools for quieting your mind is stating affirmations. Affirmations are phrases you can use to reprogram your mind. They are brief statements that put you in the proper frame of mind to accept intuitive inputs. Affirmations are a way of sending your brain a message that the desired result has already been achieved.

What you state, in the present tense, can easily be achieved.

Examples of affirmation that might be helpful:

"I am focusing on healing."

"I am learning how I want to be treated."

"I will not let the abuse take over my life."

"I have learned so much about myself."

"I like myself and deserve to be treated well."

Experiential Exercise - Affirmations

Using the examples of affirmations above, formulate some of your own affirmations below:

1)_____

2)_____

3)_____

4)_____

Practice your affirmations on a daily basis. Select one of the affirmations that you feel comfortable with and repeat the affirmation for about five minutes each day for one week.

Listen to Music

Listening to music is probably one of the easiest forms of relaxation. To benefit from the relaxation of music, select music that is soothing and that you find peaceful. To benefit the most from your music relaxation sessions, find approximately one-half hour of uninterrupted time by yourself daily.

Visualization

Visualization, also called guided imagery, can be used to reduce mental activity and manage stress. This method is used to induce deep relaxation and relieve tension. This can be read aloud to participants in a group.

Experiential Exercises – Visualization

Close your eyes and imagine yourself walking with a safe person through the forest.

You can hear the wind swishing through the trees as you walk and feel the wind gently touching your face.

You can hear birds singing and see the deep blue sky above the trees.

As you continue walking you find a small patch of grass alongside a beautiful lake.

You walk toward the lake and find yourself in the middle of the small patch of grass.

It is very quiet here, the water is perfectly calm and the grass feels soft below your feet.

You lie down on the grass so that you can feel the sun on your face.

You are completely relaxed, at peace with yourself and the world.

It is quiet and you feel yourself drifting off to sleep.

Allow your mind to take in the smells and sounds of this relaxing place.

Thought Stopping

Whenever you notice an anxiety-producing thought about the abuse entering your stream-of-consciousness, internally shout the word **STOP** to yourself.

Experiential Exercise – Thought Stopping

Close your eyes and imagine a situation in which a stressful thought often occurs. This might be a situation like talking in front of a group of people you do not know, going on a date or going to a difficult class or your part-time job. About thirty seconds after you begin to think about the situation, shout **STOP** as the thought begins to enter your consciousness. Eventually, with some practice, you will be able to imagine hearing the word **STOP** shouted inside your head.

Proper Breathing

Because breath is vital to life itself, proper breathing is very important and can even be an excellent form of stress reduction. The pace at which you breathe and the depth of your breathing are vital in relaxation and stress reduction.

When you encounter stressful situations, your breathing quickens and becomes more shallow. Proper breathing can also help to relax and quiet your body.

Diaphragmatic breathing (often called belly-breathing), in which you take in long, very deep breaths, is an especially powerful tool for relaxation. In diaphragmatic breathing, you push out your stomach and draw in a long deep breath. Then you exhale as slowly and as long as possible.

Repeat this until relaxation occurs.

Experiential Exercise – Breathing

- Pay attention to your breathing.

- Don't try to change it, but just become more aware of it. This will allow you to easily be brought into conscious awareness.

- Make note of the parts of your body or ways your mind is attempting to interfere with the natural movement of your breathing.

- If your attention wanders and takes you away from the focus on your breathing, simply bring back your attention so that you return to your focus.

- Dwell on the rise and fall of your chest as you inhale and exhale.

- Simply allow your attention to settle you and stop distracting thoughts.

Yoga

Yoga can be an excellent way to reduce stress in your life. Yoga has been practiced for thousands of years and has been shown to reduce stress, lower blood pressure, and bring a sense of calm to your mind. Yoga is a series of physical postures or poses which works to integrate your body, mind and spirit. Yoga is much more than stretching. Yoga postures help you to create balance in your body by developing strength and flexibility; they can be done quickly and in succession, or slowly to increase stamina and a sense of calm.

Progressive Relaxation

Progressive relaxation helps you to bring relaxation to all parts of your body through concentrated awareness. It allows you to actually produce relaxation by focusing self-suggestions of warmth and relaxation in specific muscle groups throughout the body.

Experiential Exercise - Progressive Relaxation

Sit in a comfortable position. Close your eyes and start to feel your body relaxing. Think of yourself as a rag doll. Let the relaxation pass through each organ and body part you have. In this exercise, start with your feet and progressively relax all the parts of your body. This will help you to manage your stress effectively. Begin by having your body progressively relax with such statements as:

"I am relaxing my feet . . . . My feet are warm . . . . My feet are relaxed."

"I am relaxing my ankle . . . . My ankles are warm . . . . My ankles are relaxed."

"I am relaxing my calves . . . . My calves are warm . . . . My calves are relaxed."

"I am relaxing my knees . . . . My knees are warm . . . . My knees are relaxed."

"I am relaxing my thighs . . . . My thighs are warm . . . . My thighs are relaxed."

Do this with the rest of your body until you are totally relaxed from your head to your feet. Block any distractions out of your mind as you concentrate on relaxing your entire body.

Meditation

Meditation is the practice of attempting to focus your attention on one thing at a time. It is a method in which you use repeated mental focus to quiet your mind, which in turn quiets your body.

In meditation, focusing on one thing allows your mind to stay concentrated and excludes all other thoughts. There are many different forms of meditation.

In meditation you can focus by repeating a word like *OM*, counting your breaths by saying *"one, two, three"* after you exhale with each breath, or gazing at an object like a candle or a piece of wood without thinking about it in words.

Nutrition

Many teens admit that during high stress periods they eat more than usual and eat less healthy foods. Poor eating and junk food contributes negatively to your reactions to stress and stressful situations.

Although there is no simple best food program to meet the needs of every person, some general guidelines follow to help you eat healthier at all times:

- Reduce the fat, salt and sugar in your diet.

- Eat a balanced diet with sufficient calories, vitamins and minerals.

- Do not eat excessive amounts.

- Reduce cholesterol consumption.

- Increase consumption of protein sources such as fish, poultry, nuts, eggs,

- lean meats and low-fat dairy products.

- Avoid alcohol consumption.

- Eat plenty of fruits and vegetables.

- Be aware of how stress affects your personal eating habits.

- Limit amounts of caffeine.

- Drink at least 6-8 glasses of water each day.

- Always eat a healthy breakfast.

- Exercise regularly.

Engage in Activities that Please You

Sometimes small, simple activities can help you to reduce the stress associated with extreme stress. These activities could include things like going to see a movie, calling friends to get together for dinner, taking a walk, playing with your dog or cat, or sitting on your back porch.

Quotations to Learn and Live By

How can you apply these quotes to your life? Write your thoughts for each of them.

"You have the ability to teach others how you want to be treated. If you tolerate abuse, ridicule or mistreatment, people will continue to treat you with disrespect." ~ **Dr. Robin**

_____

_____

_____

_____

_____

"In violence we forget who we are." ~ **Mary McCarthy**

_____

_____

_____

_____

_____

"Force is all-conquering, but its victories are short-lived." ~ **Abraham Lincoln**

_____

_____

_____

_____

_____

"Non-violence doesn't always work, but violence NEVER does." ~ **Madge Micheels-Cyrus**

_____

_____

_____

_____

_____

A Mahatma Ghandi Quotation

> *If I had no sense of humor, I would long ago have committed suicide.*
>
> ~Mahatma Ghandi

How is your sense of humor usually?

_____

_____

_____

_____

How is it affected by your incidents with violence? Describe an example.

_____

_____

_____

_____

How does being able to laugh help you through tough situations? Describe an example.

_____

_____

_____

_____

What movies, television shows or books can you count on to give you a good laugh?

_____

_____

_____

_____

SECTION VII:
Safety Plan

I have the right to live
without the fear of violence in my life.

_____
SIGNATURE

_____
DATE

Safety Plan

Teens often find themselves growing up in a fairly violent society.

As a teen, **you have the right to live without the fear of violence in your life**.

Living in an environment with violence and any type of abuse is not healthy and can harm you physically, emotionally and psychologically.

If you feel like your safety is at risk, **it is essential for you to develop a plan** to keep yourself and your loved ones safe until you can find the support you need. Developing a safety plan consists of several steps that we are including in this section.

The following pages contain a place for you to develop various aspects of YOUR safety plan. For each of the sections, please write in as much detail as you can. If you do not have the information you need, feel free to come back and finish your safety plan later.

The safety plan that follows has six primary sections including:

#1 – **What to Do to Be Safe** – This page will ask you to identify the primary resources available to help you if you are in an unsafe environment.

#2 – **Supportive, Trusted People** – This page will help you to identify those people in your life that you trust to help you if you do not feel safe.

#3 – **Leaving Safely** – This page will help you develop an escape plan for those times when you do not feel safe.

#4 – **Siblings, Relatives and/or Friends** – This page will help you explore how you can help other sibling, friends, and relatives who might also be in danger.

#5 – **School Safety** – This page will help you develop a plan for safely leaving school if you need to.

#6 – **School Support** – This page will ask you to identify those people in your school who could help you in an unsafe situation.

When you have completed this section, you will have developed a comprehensive safety plan that will help you if you find yourself in a situation in which your safety is in jeopardy.

SAFETY PLAN #1
What to Do to Be Safe

There is always the danger with written safety plans that the abuser will find it.
Keep this safety plan, along with copies of important documentation,
in a safe place, i.e., a locked drawer, trusted relative, friend or neighbor.
Be cautious not to choose locations the abuser may know to search.

IF SOME OF THE PAGES IN THIS SAFETY PLAN
ARE NOT APPLICABLE TO YOU, SKIP THEM.

Your safety (and that of your siblings and/or loved ones) is most important.
Below are some contacts you can have available to ensure your safety.

Contacts	Phone Numbers
Local Police Department	
Teen Violence Hotlines	
Teen Violence Shelter	
Domestic Violence Shelter	
School Counselor	
Spiritual or Religious Leader	
Trusted Adult	
Trusted Neighbor	
Someone who you can go to & feel safe	
Other	
Other	
Other	

SAFETY PLAN #2
Supportive, Trusted People

Who are trusted adults with whom you can confide about the abuse?

They can call the police if they are aware of any violence or anger.

Trusted Adult (name codes)	Phone Number	How Can This Person Help?

There is always the danger with written safety plans that the abuser will find it.
Keep this safety plan, along with copies of important documentation,
in a safe place, i.e., a locked drawer, trusted relative, friend or neighbor.
Be cautious not to choose locations the abuser may know to search.

SAFETY PLAN #3
Leaving Safely

Do you know how to get away to a safe place?

Write about how you would get yourself (and anyone else in trouble) away, if needed, in an emergency:

_____

_____

_____

List three places you could go and how will you get there:

1) _____

2) _____

3) _____

What would you take with you if you had to leave?

Place a check mark by those people and items in this list:

- ❐ Siblings
- ❐ Pets
- ❐ Cell phone & charger
- ❐ Spare Money
- ❐ Keys to your car
- ❐ Keys to your house
- ❐ Medicine
- ❐ Important papers
- ❐ Social Security Cards
- ❐ Driver's License

- ❐ Bankbook
- ❐ Debit Cards
- ❐ Change of clothes
- ❐ Immigration papers
- ❐ Personal items
- ❐ Glasses
- ❐ School records
- ❐ Medical records
- ❐ Other _____
- ❐ Other _____

Have the items in the same place, quickly retrievable in an emergency.

There is always the danger with written safety plans that the abuser will find it.
Keep this safety plan, along with copies of important documentation,
in a safe place, i.e., a locked drawer, trusted relative, friend or neighbor.
Be cautious not to choose locations the abuser may know to search.

SAFETY PLAN #4
Siblings, Relatives and/or Friends

If you had to, how could you take your siblings or anyone else, away from danger?
(use name codes)

_____

_____

_____

_____

_____

_____

List any potential dangers to your life or the other's lives if you do this:

_____

_____

_____

_____

_____

_____

What can you do, or will you do, to protect them?

_____

_____

_____

_____

_____

_____

There is always the danger with written safety plans that the abuser will find it.
Keep this safety plan, along with copies of important documentation,
in a safe place, i.e., a locked drawer, trusted relative, friend or neighbor.
Be cautious not to choose locations the abuser may know to search.

SAFETY PLAN #5
School Safety

The safest way to get home from school is . . .

_____
_____
_____
_____
_____
_____

If you need to leave school in an emergency, how will you get home?

_____
_____
_____
_____
_____
_____

Who are friends that you can count on to help you while you are in school?

_____
_____
_____
_____
_____
_____

*There is always the danger with written safety plans that the abuser will find it.
Keep this safety plan, along with copies of important documentation,
in a safe place, i.e., a locked drawer, trusted relative, friend or neighbor.
Be cautious not to choose locations the abuser may know to search.*

SAFETY PLAN #6
School Support

People who could help you in school . . .

Person (use name code)	**How This Person Could Help You**
Principal	
Teachers	
Coaches	
Counselors	
Social Workers	
Security	
Other	

There is always the danger with written safety plans that the abuser will find it.
Keep this safety plan, along with copies of important documentation,
in a safe place, i.e., a locked drawer, trusted relative, friend or neighbor.
Be cautious not to choose locations the abuser may know to search.

wholeperson

Whole Person Associates is the leading publisher
of training resources for professionals who empower
people to create and maintain healthy lifestyles.
Our creative resources will help you work effectively with
your clients in the areas of stress management,
wellness promotion, mental health and life skills.

Please visit us at our web site: **www.wholeperson.com**.
You can check out our entire line of products,
place an order, request our print catalog, and
sign up for our monthly special notifications.

Whole Person Associates

210 W Michigan

Duluth MN 55802

800-247-6789